USING MONEY

AGS

by

Larry Parsky, Ph.D.

AGS®

American Guidance Service, Inc.
4201 Woodland Road
Circle Pines, MN 55014-1796
1-800-328-2560

Life Skills Mathematics

Printed in the United States of America

ISBN 0–7854–0957–2 (Previously ISBN 0–86601–670–8)

Product Number 90865

A 0 9 8 7 6 5

Contents

Understanding Coins and Currency

Lesson 1

This unit is about money—coins and paper currency. The activities in this unit show you how they are used every day. Here are the coins and paper currency that are used to buy products or services.

Coins

Penny

Nickel

Dime

Quarter

Half-dollar

Paper Currency

One-dollar bill

Five-dollar bill

Ten-dollar bill

Twenty-dollar bill

Fifty-dollar bill

One hundred-dollar bill

The Exchange Value of Coins

Coins are used for money that is worth less than $1.00.

a. The smallest coin is the penny.
5 pennies = 1 nickel
10 pennies = 1 dime
25 pennies = 1 quarter
50 pennies = 1 half-dollar
100 pennies = 1 dollar

b. The next largest coin is the nickel.
1 nickel = 5 pennies
2 nickels = 1 dime
5 nickels = 1 quarter
10 nickels = 1 half-dollar
20 nickels = 1 dollar

c. The next largest coin is the dime.
1 dime = 10 pennies
1 dime = 2 nickels
2 dimes + 1 nickel = 1 quarter
5 dimes = 1 half-dollar
10 dimes = 1 dollar

d. The next largest coin is the quarter.
1 quarter = 25 pennies
1 quarter = 5 nickels
1 quarter = 2 dimes + 1 nickel
2 quarters = 1 half-dollar
4 quarters = 1 dollar

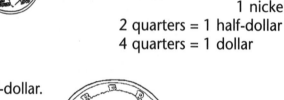

e. The next largest coin is the half-dollar.
1 half-dollar = 50 pennies
1 half-dollar = 10 nickels
1 half-dollar = 5 dimes
1 half-dollar = 2 quarters
2 half-dollars = 1 dollar

■ Write how much each coin is worth.

1. One nickel is worth

_____ pennies

2. One dime is worth

_____ pennies

_____ nickels

3. One quarter is worth

_____ pennies

_____ nickels

_____ dimes and _____ nickel

4. One half-dollar is worth

_____ pennies

_____ nickels

_____ dimes

_____ quarters

The Exchange Value of Currency

Lesson 3

Paper money is valued at $1.00 or more.

1. The smallest denomination is the one-dollar bill.
   5 one-dollar bills = 1 five-dollar bill
   10 one-dollar bills = 1 ten-dollar bill
   20 one-dollar bills = 1 twenty-dollar bill
   50 one-dollar bills = 1 fifty-dollar bill
   100 one-dollar bills = 1 one hundred-dollar bill

2. The next highest denomination is a five-dollar bill.
   1 five-dollar bill = 5 one-dollar bills
   2 five-dollar bills = 1 ten-dollar bill
   10 five-dollar bills = 1 fifty-dollar bill
   20 five-dollar bills = 1 one hundred-dollar bill

3. The next highest denomination is a ten-dollar bill.
   1 ten-dollar bill = 10 one-dollar bills
   1 ten-dollar bill = 2 five-dollar bills
   2 ten-dollar bills = 1 twenty-dollar bill
   5 ten-dollar bills = 1 fifty-dollar bill
   10 ten-dollar bills = 1 one hundred-dollar bill

4. The next highest denomination is a twenty-dollar bill.
   1 twenty-dollar bill = 20 one-dollar bills
   1 twenty-dollar bill = 4 five-dollar bills
   1 twenty-dollar bill = 2 ten-dollar bills
   2 twenty-dollar bills + 1 ten-dollar bill = 1 fifty-dollar bill
   5 twenty-dollar bills = 1 one hundred-dollar bill

5. The next highest denomination is a fifty-dollar bill.
   1 fifty-dollar bill = 50 one-dollar bills
   1 fifty-dollar bill = 10 five-dollar bills
   1 fifty-dollar bill = 5 ten-dollar bills
   2 fifty-dollar bills = 1 one hundred-dollar bill

6. The next highest denomination is a one hundred-dollar bill.
   1 one hundred-dollar bill = 100 one-dollar bills
   1 one hundred-dollar bill = 20 five-dollar bills
   1 one hundred-dollar bill = 10 ten-dollar bills
   1 one hundred-dollar bill = 5 twenty-dollar bills
   1 one hundred-dollar bill = 2 fifty-dollar bills

Knowing the Value of Money

 Write how much each bill is worth.

1. A one-dollar bill is worth

______ pennies

______ nickels

______ dimes

______ quarters

______ half-dollars

2. One five-dollar bill is worth

______ nickels

______ dimes

______ quarters

______ half-dollars

______ one-dollar bills

3. One fifty-dollar bill is worth

______ half-dollars

______ one-dollar bills

______ five-dollar bills

______ ten-dollar bills

______ twenty-dollar bills and

______ ten-dollar bill

4. One ten-dollar bill is worth

______ nickels

______ dimes

______ quarters

______ half-dollars

______ one-dollar bills

______ five-dollar bills

5. One twenty-dollar bill is worth

______ half-dollars

______ one-dollar bills

______ five-dollar bills

______ ten-dollar bills

6. One hundred-dollar bill is worth

______ one-dollar bills

______ five-dollar bills

______ ten-dollar bills

______ twenty-dollar bills

The Dollar Sign and the Decimal Point

Lesson 5

Our money system is based on units of ten. Each ten is made up of ten cents. It takes 10 tens, or 100 cents, to make $1.00. Study the chart below.

1 ten = $.10 or 10¢	1¢	1¢	1¢	1¢	1¢	1¢	1¢	1¢	1¢	1¢
2 tens = $.20 or 20¢	1¢	1¢	1¢	1¢	1¢	1¢	1¢	1¢	1¢	1¢
3 tens = $.30 or 30¢	1¢	1¢	1¢	1¢	1¢	1¢	1¢	1¢	1¢	1¢
4 tens = $.40 or 40¢	1¢	1¢	1¢	1¢	1¢	1¢	1¢	1¢	1¢	1¢
5 tens = $.50 or 50¢	1¢	1¢	1¢	1¢	1¢	1¢	1¢	1¢	1¢	1¢
6 tens = $.60 or 60¢	1¢	1¢	1¢	1¢	1¢	1¢	1¢	1¢	1¢	1¢
7 tens = $.70 or 70¢	1¢	1¢	1¢	1¢	1¢	1¢	1¢	1¢	1¢	1¢
8 tens = $.80 or 80¢	1¢	1¢	1¢	1¢	1¢	1¢	1¢	1¢	1¢	1¢
9 tens = $.90 or 90¢	1¢	1¢	1¢	1¢	1¢	1¢	1¢	1¢	1¢	1¢
10 tens = $1.00 or 100 ¢	1¢	1¢	1¢	1¢	1¢	1¢	1¢	1¢	1¢	1¢

A Use a dollar sign ($) to write the amounts of money. Money worth less than one dollar is written to the right of the decimal point (.). Study the following examples. Then, complete the chart below.

Examples:

	DOLLAR SIGN	DECIMAL POINT	DIMES	PENNIES	AMOUNT OF MONEY
Eight Cents	$	.	0	8	$.08
Twenty Cents	$	.	2	0	$.20
Thirty-seven Cents	$	.	3	7	$.37

	DOLLAR SIGN	DECIMAL POINT	DIMES	PENNIES	AMOUNT OF MONEY
1. Forty-five Cents					
2. Nineteen Cents					
3. Seventy-six Cents					
4. Thirty-three Cents					
5. Ninety-eight Cents					

UNIT 1

The dollar sign and decimal point are used to write amounts of money. The decimal point is used to separate the dollars from the cents. Money worth more than one dollar is written to the left of the decimal point. Study the following examples.

Examples:

	Dollar Sign	Hundred Dollars	Ten Dollars	One Dollar	.	Dimes	Pennies
Two dollars	$			2	.	0	0
Ten dollars	$		1	0	.	0	0
One hundred dollars	$	1	0	0	.	0	0
Two hundred fifty-five dollars	$	2	5	5	.	0	0
Forty dollars and twelve cents	$		4	0	.	1	2
Five hundred seventy dollars	$	5	7	0	.	0	0

B Use a dollar sign and a decimal point to write the following amounts of money. Study the examples above. Then, complete the chart.

6. Nine dollars and fifty-two cents
7. Seventeen dollars and ninety-three cents
8. Thirty dollars and forty cents
9. Fourteen dollars and ninety-three cents
10. Fifty-seven dollars and eighty-five cents
11. One hundred fifty dollars and ten cents
12. Four hundred two dollars and eighty cents
13. One hundred twelve dollars and seventeen cents
14. Five hundred thirty-three dollars and four cents
15. Seven hundred sixty-two dollars

Dollar Sign	Hundred Dollars	Ten Dollars	One Dollar	.	Dimes	Pennies
6.						
7.						
8.						
9.						
10.						
11.						
12.						
13.						
14.						
15.						

Counting Coins

Write out the numerical value of these coins. Study the following example. Include the dollar sign ($) and the decimal point (.) in each answer.

Example:

$.50

1.

1. 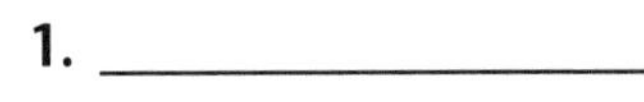

2.

2. 

3.

3. ____________________

4.

4. ____________________

5.

5. ____________________

6.

6. ____________________

UNIT 1

Understanding Money

A Write how much money the following coins are worth. Study the example.

Example: 7 nickels $.35

1. 4 dimes ________
2. 25 pennies ________
3. 9 quarters ________
4. 12 nickels ________
5. 2 half-dollars ________
6. 13 dimes ________
7. 11 nickels ________
8. 7 half-dollars ________
9. 99 pennies ________
10. 10 quarters ________
11. 15 dimes ________
12. 5 half-dollars ________

B Write how much money the following bills are worth. Study the example.

Example: 6 ten-dollar bills $60.00

13. 9 one-dollar bills ________
14. 5 five-dollar bills ________
15. 8 ten-dollar bills ________
16. 40 one-dollar bills ________
17. 8 five-dollar bills ________
18. 29 one-dollar bills ________
19. 9 five-dollar bills ________
20. 70 one-dollar bills ________
21. 16 five-dollar bills ________
22. 6 five-dollar bills ________

C Write the following amounts of money in numbers. Study the example.

Example: Six dollars and twenty-eight cents $6.28

23. Two dollars and eighty-four cents ________
24. Seventeen dollars and forty-five cents ________
25. Eighty dollars and nineteen cents ________
26. Fifty-one dollars and five cents ________
27. One hundred fifty dollars and forty-two cents ________
28. Seventy-four dollars and thirty-six cents ________

Matching Currency

 Match each set of currency with the correct amount of money. Write the letter of your answer on the line beside each amount at the bottom of the page.

A.

B.

C.

D.

E.

1. $3.00 ____ 2. $5.00 ____ 3. $9.00 ____ 4. $20.00 ____ 5. $12.00 ____

More Matching Currency

Match each set of currency with the correct amount of money. Write the letter of your answer beside the amount at the bottom of the page.

A.

B.

C.

D.

E.

1. \$30.00 ____ 2. \$15.00 ____ 3. \$50.00 ____ 4. \$8.00 ____ 5. \$16.00 ____

Counting Currency

Write out the numerical value of these bills. Study the following example. Remember to write the dollar sign ($) and the decimal point (.) in your answer.

Example:

$12.00

1.

1. ______________

2.

2. ______________

3.

3. ______________

Count the Currency

 Write out the numerical value of these bills. Study the following example. Write the dollar sign ($) and the decimal point (.) in your answer.

Example:

$24.00

1.

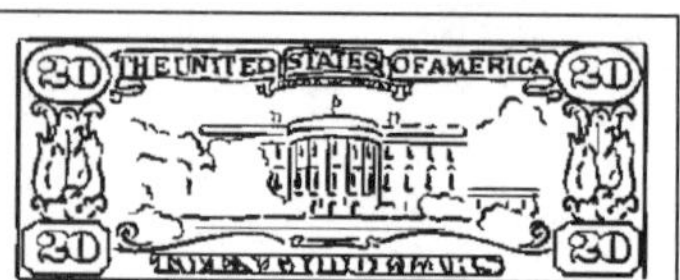

1. 

2.

2. 

3.

3. ____________________

Matching Money

Match each set of currency and coins with the correct amount of money. Write the letter of your answer on the line beside each amount at the bottom of the page.

A.

B.

C.

D.

E.

1. $2.25 ____ 2. $1.07 ____ 3. $1.30 ____ 4. $2.15____ 5. $5.50 ____

Match the Money

Match each set of currency and coins with an amount of money. Write the letter of your answer on the line beside each amount at the bottom of the page.

A.

B.

C.

D.

E.

1. $10.15 ____   2. $15.25 ____   3. $20.75 ____   4. $6.45 ____   5. $3.60 ____

Counting Money

Write out the numerical value of these coins and bills. Study the following example. Include the dollar sign ($) and the decimal point (.) in each answer.

Example:

$2.50

1.

1. ____________

2.

2. ____________

3.

3. ____________

Money Chart—Counting Coins

This is a money chart for counting coins. Part of the chart has been completed. The number of coins is shown in the first column. Write the amount of money you would have if you had that many coins of each value.

Number of Coins	Pennies	Nickels	Dimes	Quarters	Half Dollars
1	$.01	$.05		$.25	
2			$.20	$.50	$1.00
3	$.03		$.30		
4	$.04	$.20		$1.00	$2.00
5	$.05	$.25	$.50	$1.25	$2.50
6			$.60		
7					$3.50
8			$.80		
9					
10	$.10	$.50	$1.00	$2.50	$5.00
11				$2.75	
12		$.60	$1.20	$3.00	
13		$.65	$1.30		
14		$.70			
15	$.15		$1.50		
16				$4.00	$8.00
17		$.85			
18		$.90			
19	$.19		$1.90	$4.75	
20	$.20				$10.00

Money Chart—Counting Currency

This is a money chart for counting currency. Part of the chart has been completed. The number of bills is shown in the first column. Write the amount of money you would have if you had that many bills of each value.

Number of Bills	One-Dollar Bill(s)	Five-Dollar Bill(s)	Ten-Dollar Bill(s)	Twenty-Dollar Bill(s)	Fifty-Dollar Bill(s)	One Hundred-Dollar Bill(s)
1	$1.00	$5.00	$10.00	$20.00	$50.00	$100.00
2	$2.00	$10.00		$40.00	$100.00	$200.00
3	$3.00		$30.00			
4		$20.00		$80.00	$200.00	$400.00
5	$5.00	$25.00	$50.00	$100.00	$250.00	$500.00
6				$120.00		
7	$7.00	$35.00	$70.00		$350.00	
8				$160.00		$800.00
9	$9.00	$45.00	$90.00		$450.00	
10	$10.00		$100.00	$200.00		$1,000.00
11		$55.00			$550.00	$1,100.00
12	$12.00		$120.00			$1,200.00
13				$260.00	$650.00	$1,300.00
14	$14.00	$70.00	$140.00			$1,400.00
15	$15.00			$300.00	$750.00	$1,500.00
16			$160.00			
17		$85.00		$340.00	$850.00	$1,700.00
18	$18.00		$180.00			
19					$950.00	
20	$20.00			$400.00	$1,000.00	$2,000.00

UNIT 1

The Value of Coins

Lesson 17

A Find the value of the following coins. Study the examples. Write each answer on the line.

Examples: 14 pennies = $.14 6 nickels = $.30

1. 3 dimes = ____________
2. 2 quarters = ____________
3. 6 nickels = ____________
4. 29 pennies = ____________
5. 3 quarters = ____________
6. 4 dimes = ____________
7. 7 nickels = ____________
8. 25 pennies = ____________
9. 4 quarters = ____________
10. 9 nickels = ____________
11. 5 quarters = ____________
12. 10 dimes = ____________
13. 18 nickels = ____________
14. 100 pennies = ____________
15. 17 dimes = ____________
16. 20 nickels = ____________
17. 7 quarters = ____________
18. 75 pennies = ____________
19. 30 dimes = ____________
20. 12 nickels = ____________

B Use a calculator to find the value of the following coins.

21. 7 dimes = ____________
22. 11 nickels = ____________
23. 6 quarters = ____________
24. 8 dimes = ____________
25. 51 pennies = ____________
26. 8 quarters = ____________
27. 15 dimes = ____________
28. 14 nickels = ____________
29. 20 dimes = ____________
30. 9 quarters = ____________

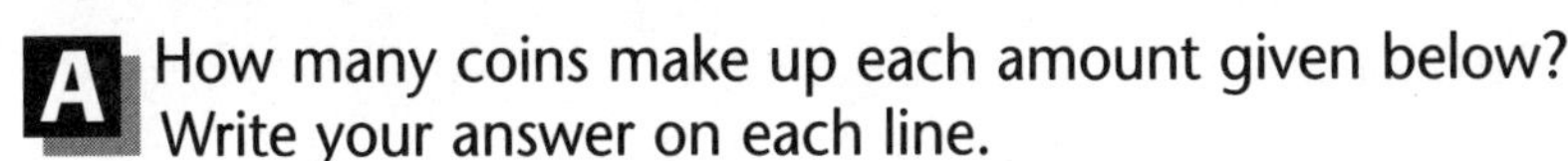

The Value of Money

Lesson 18

UNIT 1

A How many coins make up each amount given below? Write your answer on each line.

1. $3.00 = ______________ quarters
2. $1.00 = ______________ nickels
3. $5.00 = ______________ pennies
4. $2.50 = ______________ half-dollars
5. $4.75 = ______________ quarters
6. $2.10 = ______________ dimes
7. $7.50 = ______________ half-dollars
8. $1.50 = ______________ quarters
9. $8.00 = ______________ dimes
10. $1.50 = ______________ nickels
11. $1.10 = ______________ dimes
12. $2.25 = ______________ quarters
13. $2.00 = ______________ nickels
14. $5.00 = ______________ quarters
15. $3.90 = ______________ dimes
16. $8.00 = ______________ half-dollars
17. $10.00 = ______________ quarters
18. $12.00 = ______________ dimes

B Read each problem carefully. Solve the problems and write your answers on the lines.

19. Anthony wants to exchange his paper currency for quarters. How many quarters can he get for $9.50? ______________

20. The gumball machine in Mr. Gomez's store takes only dimes. Mr. Gomez removed $6.70 from the machine. How many dimes were there? ______________

UNIT 1

Find the Value

A Find the value of each set of coins. Study the example. Write your answer on each line.

Example: 2 dimes and 1 quarter = $.45

1. 3 pennies and 1 quarter = ____________

2. 2 pennies and 2 dimes = ____________

3. 3 nickels and 1 quarter = ____________

4. 4 dimes and 1 half-dollar = ____________

5. 2 dimes and 1 quarter = ____________

6. 3 pennies and 4 nickels = ____________

7. 1 quarter and 1 half-dollar = ____________

8. 2 nickels and 2 quarters = ____________

9. 3 nickels and 4 dimes = ____________

10. 5 dimes and 1 quarter = ____________

11. 3 nickels and 1 half-dollar = ____________

12. 3 quarters and 1 half-dollar = ____________

B Use a calculator to find the value of each set of coins.

13. 5 nickels and 5 dimes = ____________

14. 10 dimes and 2 quarters = ____________

15. 1 dime and 4 quarters = ____________

16. 10 pennies and 2 half-dollars = ____________

Making Change

 Draw a picture of the coins being described. Study the example.

Example: 2 coins that make $.20 = 

1. 3 coins that make $.25 = ____________
2. 3 coins that make $.30 = ____________
3. 4 coins that make $.20 = ____________
4. 2 coins that make $.35 = ____________
5. 4 coins that make $1.00 = ____________
6. 2 coins that make $.15 = ____________
7. 3 coins that make $.45 = ____________
8. 5 coins that make $.40 = ____________
9. 3 coins that make $.40 = ____________
10. 2 coins that make $1.00 = ____________
11. 3 coins that make $.75 = ____________
12. 6 coins that make $.10 = ____________
13. 2 coins that make $.30 = ____________
14. 7 coins that make $.15 = ____________
15. 5 coins that make $.25 = ____________
16. 2 coins that make $.55 = ____________

UNIT 1

Making Change Practice

Lesson 21

Malailea gave the following amounts of change to customers. For each item, write two different ways she could have made change. The first problem has been done for you.

1. $.75 3 quarters; 7 dimes, 1 nickel
2. $.25 ____
3. $.86 ____
4. $.50 ____
5. $.95 ____
6. $.37 ____
7. $.71 ____
8. $.48 ____
9. $1.06 ____
10. $.12 ____
11. $.05 ____
12. $.42 ____
13. $20.50 ____
14. $15.51 ____
15. $5.25 ____
16. $11.00 ____
17. $1.50 ____
18. $85.00 ____
19. $.90 ____
20. $8.05 ____

The Value of Coins and Currency

A Find the value of each set of coins and paper currency. Study the example. Write your answer on each line.

Example: 1 nickel, 1 quarter, and 2 one-dollar bills = $2.30

1. 4 dimes and 5 one-dollar bills = ____________
2. 1 quarter and 1 ten-dollar bill = ____________
3. 1 half-dollar and 1 five-dollar bill = ____________
4. 2 quarters and 1 twenty-dollar bill = ____________
5. 1 quarter, 1 half-dollar, and 1 ten-dollar bill = ____________
6. 3 quarters and 2 one-dollar bills = ____________
7. 1 nickel, 1 quarter, and 4 one-dollar bills = ____________
8. 1 nickel, 1 half-dollar, and 2 five-dollar bills = ____________
9. 5 dimes, 1 one-dollar bill, and 1 ten-dollar bill = ____________
10. 1 quarter, 1 five-dollar bill, and 1 twenty-dollar bill = ____________

B Read each problem carefully. Solve the problems and write your answers on the lines.

11. Mario has 1 half-dollar, 1 five-dollar bill, and 1 ten-dollar bill. How much money does he have in all? ____________

12. Charlene gave the grocery store clerk 3 dimes, 1 one-dollar bill, and 1 five-dollar bill. How much money did she pay in all? ____________

REVIEW

Review: Unit 1

A Write the numerical value of each set of coins and bills.

1.

1. ______________

2.

2. ______________

3.

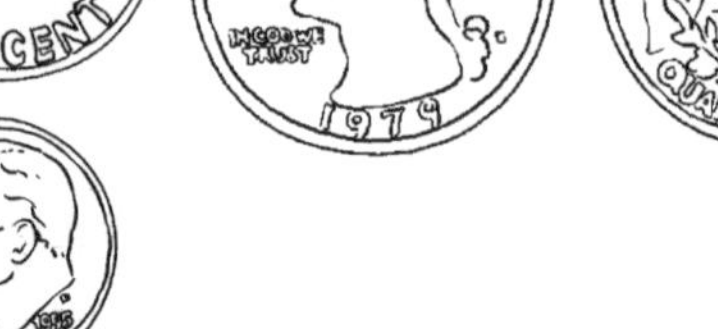

3. ______________

4.

4. ______________

REVIEW

B Write how much money the following coins are worth.

5. 6 dimes ___________
6. 20 pennies ___________
7. 5 quarters ___________
8. 16 nickels ___________
9. 4 half-dollars ___________
10. 5 nickels ___________
11. 15 dimes ___________
12. 10 nickels ___________
13. 6 half-dollars ___________
14. 88 pennies ___________
15. 8 quarters ___________
16. 15 nickels ___________

C Write how much money the following paper currency is worth.

17. 8 one-dollar bills ___________
18. 3 twenty-dollar bills ___________
19. 9 ten-dollar bills ___________
20. 20 one-dollar bills ___________
21. 6 five-dollar bills ___________
22. 19 one-dollar bills ___________
23. 5 ten-dollar bills ___________
24. 50 one-dollar bills ___________
25. 12 five-dollar bills ___________
26. 4 twenty-dollar bills ___________

D Write the following amounts of money in numbers.

27. Five dollars and thirty-seven cents ___________
28. Eight dollars and fifty-five cents ___________
29. Fifteen dollars and sixty cents ___________
30. Ninety dollars and eighteen cents ___________
31. Forty-one dollars and nine cents ___________
32. Two hundred seventy-five dollars and sixty-six cents ___________

Money Symbols

This chapter will give you practice in solving math problems that involve money. Money problems have two important symbols—the dollar sign and the decimal point.

The dollar sign ($) is used to indicate money. Put it in front of the first number of the problem and the first number of the answer. Study the following examples.

$$\begin{array}{r} \$122.55 \\ \underline{+\ 61.00} \\ \$183.55 \end{array} \qquad \begin{array}{r} \$547.72 \\ \underline{-\ 132.31} \\ \$415.41 \end{array} \qquad \begin{array}{r} \$100.00 \\ \underline{\times \quad 2.00} \\ \$200.00 \end{array} \qquad \begin{array}{r} \$213 \\ 2\overline{)\$426} \\ \underline{-4} \\ 2 \\ \underline{-2} \\ 6 \\ \underline{-6} \\ 0 \end{array}$$

The decimal point (.) separates dollars from cents. It is read as "and." For example, $132.75 is read as "One hundred thirty-two dollars *and* seventy-five cents." The numbers to the right of the decimal point are cents. The numbers to the left of the decimal point are dollars.

The decimal point is an important symbol. Leaving out the decimal point in a problem is a big error. Look at the following examples: $5.76 and $576.00. The decimal point shows that the first amount is less than the second amount.

Adding Change

These problems have dollar signs and decimal points in the addends. When you add money, the dollar sign and the decimal point must be placed in the sum. Decimal points must be lined up one under the other. The first one is done for you.

Example:

$ .21 ← Addend
.05 ← Addend
+ .30 ← Addend
$ .56 ← Sum

A Add.

1. $.25 .15 + .10	**2.** $.13 .22 + .44	**3.** $.03 .12 + .31	**4.** $.51 .05 + .21	**5.** $.24 .32 + .43
6. $.14 .26 + .09	**7.** $.25 .18 + .37	**8.** $.49 .06 + .30	**9.** $.38 .07 + .45	**10.** $.15 .24 + .29
11. $.54 .63 + .42	**12.** $.41 .25 + .40	**13.** $.72 .43 + .86	**14.** $.40 .55 + .63	**15.** $.92 .50 + .36
16. $.86 .35 + .18	**17.** $.07 .55 + .86	**18.** $.79 .48 + .15	**19.** $.37 .09 + .61	**20.** $.85 .26 + .69

B Use a calculator to solve the following problems.

21. $.95 .12 + .36	**22.** $.25 .38 + .96	**23.** $.49 .84 + .50	**24.** $.61 .20 + .39	**25.** $.58 .19 + .48
26. $.26 .35 + .29	**27.** $.30 .46 + .92	**28.** $.15 .29 + .08	**29.** $.88 .49 + .65	**30.** $.50 .86 + .92

Adding Money

The following problems have dollar signs and decimal points. To correctly solve each problem, place the dollar sign and the decimal point in the answer. Line decimal points up one under the other.

 Add.

1. $2.00 + .83	2. $1.20 + 3.45	3. $5.43 + 3.20	4. $1.34 + 1.15	5. $4.36 + .41
6. $1.69 + 1.08	7. $2.25 + 1.28	8. $3.38 + 4.05	9. $4.59 + .18	10. $5.08 + .26
11. $4.40 + 1.42	12. $1.82 + 1.40	13. $2.50 + .34	14. $1.81 + 2.03	15. $3.84 + .98
16. $5.21 + 8.20	17. $8.30 + 1.04	18. $7.55 + 8.03	19. $4.03 + 9.50	20. $2.41 + 9.23

B Read each problem carefully. Solve it on a separate sheet of paper. Write your answer on the line beside each problem.

21. Anna bought items at the hardware store that cost $6.78 and $8.16. How much did the two items cost in all? __________

22. Juan's restaurant bill was $7.99. He added a tip of $1.88. How much did he pay altogether? __________

Addition Problems

When you add money, the dollar sign and the decimal point must be placed in the answer. Be sure to line up decimal points one under the other.

A Add.

1.	2.	3.	4.	5.
\$10.34	\$22.13	\$12.41	\$43.24	\$31.23
12.13	10.34	4.12	12.32	3.50
+ 3.20	+ 15.01	+ 3.12	+ 10.10	+ 40.12

6.	7.	8.	9.	10.
\$24.35	\$13.42	\$13.18	\$40.25	\$12.42
1.26	20.15	21.35	21.23	31.29
+ 10.13	+ 2.25	+ 32.13	+ 13.19	+ 40.16

11.	12.	13.	14.	15.
\$12.43	\$22.24	\$10.53	\$32.15	\$22.50
3.28	5.85	53.82	41.80	30.69
+ 11.45	+ 21.36	+ 2.86	+ 13.56	+ 3.26

16.	17.	18.	19.	20.
\$24.45	\$15.95	\$21.63	\$51.34	\$24.95
13.46	12.88	15.72	26.85	15.76
+ 12.53	+ 1.75	+ 3.15	+ 14.46	+ 8.48

B Use a calculator to solve the following problems.

21.	22.	23.	24.	25.
\$43.29	\$23.75	\$16.29	\$35.76	\$88.35
34.62	12.88	15.72	26.85	40.93
+ 42.16	+ 13.17	+ 64.32	+ 54.25	+ 7.46

26.	27.	28.	29.	30.
\$32.85	\$48.75	\$80.58	\$30.18	\$40.81
23.92	10.98	94.75	63.09	32.97
+ 2.18	+ 36.64	+ 25.17	+ 26.24	+ 53.06

UNIT 2

Add the Money

When you add money, the dollar sign and the decimal point must be placed in the answer. Be sure to line up decimal points one under the other.

A Add.

1.	2.	3.	4.	5.
$124.50	$223.51	$323.40	$121.41	$121.04
52.23	20.05	5.16	60.42	514.50
+ 4.10	+ 15.20	+ 221.38	+ 414.10	+ 62.35

6.	7.	8.	9.	10.
$134.29	$423.25	$220.39	$330.15	$523.69
40.10	33.27	30.29	132.48	124.03
+ 100.39	+ 231.42	+ 134.16	+ 36.06	+ 301.24

11.	12.	13.	14.	15.
$220.58	$151.88	$450.62	$236.73	$370.68
103.82	43.73	200.38	140.36	215.97
+ 52.95	+ 2.25	+ 45.79	+ 120.51	+ 402.19

16.	17.	18.	19.	20.
$129.27	$621.12	$350.50	$515.34	$213.95
5.63	43.63	125.19	36.72	501.86
+ 250.72	+ 204.25	+ 19.48	+ 401.26	+ 52.63

B Read each problem carefully. Solve it on a separate sheet of paper. Write your answer on the line beside each problem.

21. Margaret paid bills of $425.72, $40.31, and $185.88. How much did she pay in all? __________

22. Construction bills for Ricardo's new family room were $752.86, $309.75, and $180.32. What was the total of the construction bills? __________

Addition—Horizontal, Part 1

An addition problem is sometimes written *horizontally* (side by side). To find the sum, rewrite the problem. Put the **pennies** under the pennies, the **dimes** under the dimes, and the **one-dollars** under the one-dollars. Decimal points must be lined up one under the other. Put the dollar sign and the decimal point in each answer. Study the example.

Example:

One-dollars / Dimes / Pennies

$1.28 + $.98 + $.06 = $2.32

```
 $1.28  ←— Addend
   .98  ←— Addend
 + .06  ←— Addend
 $2.32  ←— Sum
```

A Rewrite each problem. Add. Then check your answer.

1. $.16 + $.23 + $.50 =

2. $18 + $.26 + $.38 =

3. $.97 + $.48 + $.76 =

4. $4.03 + $.42 + $5.06 =

5. $1.24 + $3.06 + $1.55 =

6. $2.85 + $1.99 + $3.06 =

UNIT 2

Addition—Horizontal, Part 2

An addition problem is sometimes written horizontally (side by side). To find the sum, rewrite the problem. Put the **pennies** under the pennies, the **dimes** under the dimes, the **one-dollars** under the one-dollars, and the **ten-dollars** under the ten-dollars. Decimal points must be lined up one under the other. Put the dollar sign and the decimal point in each answer. Study the example.

Example:

Ten-dollars, One-dollars, Dimes, Pennies

$38.95 + $9.48 + $.97 = $49.40

```
 $38.95  ← Addend
   9.48  ← Addend
 +  .97  ← Addend
 $49.40  ← Sum
```

B Rewrite each problem. Add. Then check your answer.

7. $1.02 + $3.50 + $1.34 =

10. $5.97 + $4.75 + $7.98 =

8. $3.28 + $.09 + $1.25 =

11. $20.14 + $33.54 + $12.08 =

9. $1.66 + $2.68 + $4.05 =

12. $30.49 + $2.88 + $51.95 =

Subtracting Money

The following problems have dollar signs and decimal points. To correctly solve each problem, the dollar sign and the decimal point must be placed in the answer. Decimal points should be lined up one under the other.

A Subtract.

1. $5.83 − 3.10
2. $8.75 − 8.34
3. $7.56 − 3.23
4. $4.63 − 2.61
5. $9.78 − 5.02
6. $3.62 − .40
7. $6.85 − .82
8. $2.75 − .25
9. $5.96 − .71
10. $8.94 − .92
11. $8.51 − 4.46
12. $6.30 − 5.18
13. $4.56 − 1.08
14. $2.25 − .66
15. $7.06 − 3.58
16. $9.03 − 1.21
17. $4.28 − 2.43
18. $7.45 − 6.90
19. $3.09 − 1.85
20. $8.17 − 7.83

B Read each problem carefully. Solve it on a separate sheet of paper. Write your answer on the line beside each problem.

21. Alicia had $9.00. She spent $2.78 at the drugstore. How much did she have left? ________________

22. Carlos had $3.59 in his pocket. He gave his son $2.80. How much money did he have left? ________________

Subtraction Problems

When you subtract money, the dollar sign and the decimal point must be placed in the answer. Be sure to line up decimal points one under the other.

 Subtract.

1. $47.23 − 25.20
2. $38.75 − 21.42
3. $76.58 − 22.52
4. $34.84 − 30.51
5. $93.68 − 63.23
6. $38.46 − 5.42
7. $85.77 − 3.20
8. $56.59 − 6.13
9. $29.64 − 5.01
10. $67.85 − 3.21
11. $56.83 − 51.25
12. $73.50 − 41.19
13. $48.36 − 25.28
14. $84.67 − 43.09
15. $48.72 − 30.63
16. $43.26 − 22.74
17. $25.17 − 10.82
18. $68.09 − 24.15
19. $76.73 − 35.83
20. $81.46 − 40.80

B Use a calculator to solve the following problems.

21. $70.63 − 25.41
22. $32.76 − 24.62
23. $86.94 − 58.03
24. $53.18 − 35.05
25. $61.84 − 29.62
26. $42.23 − 38.47
27. $73.00 − 54.26
28. $97.28 − 58.79
29. $82.03 − 25.74
30. $83.10 − 75.63

Subtract the Money

When you subtract money, the dollar sign and the decimal point must be placed in the answer. Be sure to line up decimal points one under the other.

A Subtract.

1. $256.72 – 102.71	2. $475.99 – 203.20	3. $674.85 – 613.22	4. $846.48 – 32.02	5. $573.26 – 302.14
6. $573.43 – 102.25	7. $329.70 – 219.53	8. $176.52 – 30.29	9. $794.14 – 721.07	10. $625.36 – 413.08
11. $923.26 – 812.68	12. $273.05 – 31.89	13. $399.41 – 208.59	14. $464.00 – 360.95	15. $785.32 – 641.69
16. $643.21 – 328.56	17. $830.63 – 605.89	18. $543.00 – 436.83	19. $280.00 – 35.89	20. $761.24 – 405.68
21. $345.12 – 286.36	22. $400.00 – 123.78	23. $918.72 – 629.95	24. $740.85 – 36.97	25. $312.42 – 259.86

B Read each problem carefully. Solve it on a separate sheet of paper. Write your answer on the line beside each problem.

26. Lee made $247.30 at her garage sale. She spent $36.21 for advertising and refreshments. What was her total profit? __________

27. Michael and Beth have a furniture budget of $675.00. Their new chair cost $273.84. How much do they have left? __________

28. Andy got two estimates on a roof repair for his house. The first estimate was $198.75; the second was for $237.90. What was the cost difference between the two estimates? __________

Subtraction Word Problems

Lesson 10

Sometimes you will need to solve several subtraction problems in order to find out how much money is left. Remember to line up the decimal points one under the other, and place a decimal point in your answer. Study the example and complete the problems.

Example: Shawna took $42.10 with her to the store. She bought milk for $1.73, cereal for $3.97, hamburger meat for $4.78, buns for $2.59, and paper cups for $1.09. How much money did Shawna have after buying these items?

$$
\begin{array}{r}
\$42.10 \\
-\ 1.73 \\
\hline
40.37 \\
-\ 3.97 \\
\hline
36.40 \\
-\ 4.78 \\
\hline
31.62 \\
-\ 2.59 \\
\hline
29.03 \\
-\ 1.09 \\
\hline
\$27.94
\end{array}
$$

Shawna had $27.94 after buying groceries.

1. Max's checkbook balance is $979.84. He has to spend $198.17 to repair his car, and he wants to buy a bicycle for his sister that costs $239.98. How much money will he have left after making these purchases? __________

2. The Science Club raised $327.10 at an auction. The club officers plan to buy a microscope for $127.49, two boxes of slides for $12.99 each, a used film projector for $80.00, and an atlas for $39.95. How much money will the club have left after buying these supplies? __________

3. Mr. Harvey charges each customer $100.00 for weekly landscaping and lawn care. He pays $48.00 to his employees; $19.78 goes toward equipment maintenance; and $15.04 is spent on gasoline, fertilizer, and other supplies. To figure Mr. Harvey's profit, find out how much money is left after he pays his expenses? __________

4. Rachel has $137.48 saved in her coin bank. She used $105.00 to buy an outfit; then she bought lunch for $4.95 and some flowers for $12.79. How much money did she have left? __________

UNIT 2

5. Antonio's bank statement showed that he had $1,000.00 in his savings account at the beginning of the month. On the 12th, he transferred $159.00 to his checking account, and on the 19th, he transferred $98.95 to checking. On the 25th, $149.21 was automatically withdrawn from his savings to pay for health insurance. How much did Antonio have left in his savings account after these withdrawals? ________

6. Kyoko received a scholarship of $10,500 for art school. The scholarship will pay for tuition, room and board, and art supplies and other expenses. Tuition at the school is $6,500.00 and the charge for a room and meals is $2,115.75. How much money does Kyoko have to spend on her supplies? ________

7. Claudia had $75.00 to spend on birthday presents for her three granddaughters. She bought a sweater for $19.39, a book of photographs for $22.95, and a pair of skates for $27.50. How much did she have left? ________

8. Marcus has $800.00 to spend on new office equipment and supplies. He is planning to buy two filing cabinets for $79.95 each and three bookcases for $105.15 each. He has already ordered two boxes of paper for $43.00 each. How much money will he have left after he makes these purchases? ________

9. The Special Events Committee has $750.00 to spend on a barbecue. They have hired a band for $400.00. They have spent $169.15 on food and $45.78 on paper supplies. How much money is left in the fund? ________

10. Brad borrowed $500.00 from his brother Ron to help pay his college expenses. Brad bought books for $174.86, a calculator for $38.10, a backpack for $29.98, and computer disks for $6.03. How much of the loan is left? ________

UNIT 2

Subtraction—Horizontal, Part 1

A subtraction problem is sometimes written horizontally (side by side). To find the *difference* (answer), rewrite the problem. Put the **pennies** under the pennies, the **dimes** under the dimes, the **one-dollars** under the one-dollars, and so on. Decimal points must be lined up one under the other. Put the dollar sign and the decimal point in each answer. Study the example.

Example:

$50.00 – $6.78 = $43.22

Ten-dollars, One-dollars, Dimes, Pennies

$50.00	← **Minuend**
– 6.78	← **Subtrahend**
$43.22	← **Difference**

Check:

$6.78	← **Subtrahend**
+ 43.22	← **Difference**
$50.00	← **Minuend**

A Rewrite each problem. Subtract. Then check each answer.

1. $4.65 – $3.62 =

2. $5.24 – $1.06 =

3. $7.15 – $2.86 =

4. $32.53 – $10.12 =

5. $25.48 – $23.86 =

6. $46.13 – $23.86 =

UNIT 2

Subtraction—Horizontal, Part 2

When you subtract money, be sure to line up the decimal points. Put the dollar sign and the decimal point in each answer.

Example:

$422.00 – $75.13 = $346.87

Hundred-dollars, Ten-dollars, One-dollars, Dimes, Pennies

```
 $422.00  ← Minuend
 – 75.13  ← Subtrahend
 $346.87  ← Difference
```

Check:

```
  $75.13  ← Subtrahend
+ 346.87  ← Difference
 $422.00  ← Minuend
```

B Rewrite each problem. Subtract. Then check each answer.

7. $995.58 – $893.15 =

8. $536.24 – $203.16 =

9. $859.13 – $605.57 =

10. $346.70 – $128.51 =

11. $657.24 – $168.96 =

12. $470.51 – $268.36 =

U N I T 2

Subtraction—Horizontal, Part 3

When you subtract money, be sure to line up the decimal points. Put the dollar sign and the decimal point in each answer.

Example:

$4,024.14 – $188.75 = $3,835.39

Thousand-dollars | Hundred-dollars | Ten-dollars | One-dollars | Dimes | Pennies

$4,024.14	← Minuend
– 188.75	← Subtrahend
$3,835.39	← Difference

Check:

$188.75	← Subtrahend
+ 3,835.39	← Difference
$4,024.14	← Minuend

C Rewrite each problem. Subtract. Then check each answer.

13. $2,634.26 – $1,324.13 =

14. $8,653.70 – $2,310.68 =

15. $4,884.24 – $723.89 =

16. $5,631.42 – $2,316.95 =

17. $6,743.00 – $1,387.48 =

18. $7,564.24 – $4,895.78 =

Multiplying Change

In these problems, you will multiply money by whole numbers. Each problem has a dollar sign and a decimal point. The product must also have a dollar sign and a decimal point. Since there are two decimal places in the multiplicand, count two decimal places in the product. Study the example and complete the problems.

Example:

$$\begin{array}{r} \$.23 \leftarrow \text{multiplicand} \\ \underline{\times\ 3} \leftarrow \text{multiplier} \\ \$.69 \end{array}$$

 Multiply.

1. $.28 x 8	2. $.30 x 3	3. $.41 x 2	4. $.13 x 3	5. $.21 x 4
6. $.15 x 5	7. $.25 x 3	8. $.17 x 2	9. $.29 x 3	10. $.38 x 2
11. $.41 x 5	12. $.80 x 9	13. $.52 x 3	14. $.72 x 2	15. $.60 x 5
16. $.34 x 5	17. $.85 x 4	18. $.46 x 8	19. $.63 x 7	20. $.95 x 6
21. $.13 x 5	22. $.40 x 4	23. $.99 x 6	24. $.32 x 3	25. $.72 x 5
26. $.20 x 5	27. $.15 x 6	28. $.21 x 4	29. $.85 x 5	30. $.30 x 7

UNIT 2

Multiplication—Single Multipliers, Part 1

Lesson 13

In these problems, you will multiply money by whole numbers. Each problem has a dollar sign and a decimal point. The product must also have a dollar sign and a decimal point. Since there are two decimal places in the multiplicand, count two decimal places in the product.

A Multiply.

1. $1.03 x 3	2. $2.43 x 2	3. $4.03 x 2	4. $2.11 x 4	5. $3.20 x 3
6. $2.19 x 3	7. $1.28 x 2	8. $3.05 x 3	9. $4.25 x 2	10. $1.08 x 9
11. $2.43 x 4	12. $3.59 x 2	13. $1.76 x 3	14. $1.35 x 4	15. $2.75 x 3
16. $7.85 x 3	17. $6.46 x 5	18. $5.96 x 3	19. $8.75 x 6	20. $9.84 x 8

B Use a calculator to solve the following problems.

21. $2.51 x 4	22. $4.80 x 4	23. $8.23 x 2	24. $7.86 x 6	25. $5.08 x 9
26. $3.04 x 5	27. $5.50 x 6	28. $9.15 x 4	29. $6.95 x 7	30. $4.76 x 3

Multiplication—Single Multipliers, Part 2

UNIT 2

In these problems, you will multiply money by whole numbers. Each problem has a dollar sign and a decimal point. The product must also have a dollar sign and a decimal point. Since there are two decimal places in the multiplicand, count two decimal places in the product.

C Multiply.

31. $12.41 x 2
32. $20.31 x 3
33. $14.23 x 2
34. $11.20 x 4
35. $30.20 x 3
36. $28.16 x 2
37. $10.15 x 5
38. $40.15 x 4
39. $32.17 x 3
40. $23.49 x 2
41. $32.94 x 3
42. $21.75 x 4
43. $12.65 x 2
44. $10.46 x 5
45. $41.87 x 2
46. $45.76 x 2
47. $14.45 x 6
48. $23.24 x 4
49. $16.73 x 5
50. $26.94 x 3

D Use a calculator to solve the following problems.

51. $83.46 x 5
52. $65.84 x 4
53. $17.26 x 7
54. $59.95 x 2
55. $64.86 x 3
56. $22.56 x 3
57. $42.09 x 2
58. $35.45 x 5
59. $17.53 x 4
60. $30.16 x 7

UNIT 2

Multiplication—Single Multipliers, Part 3

In these problems, you will multiply money by whole numbers. Each problem has a dollar sign and a decimal point. The product must also have a dollar sign and a decimal point. Since there are two decimal places in the multiplicand, count two decimal places in the product.

E Multiply.

61. \$112.34 x 2	**62.** \$202.31 x 3	**63.** \$115.10 x 5	**64.** \$220.21 x 4
65. \$212.05 x 4	**66.** \$313.24 x 3	**67.** \$101.06 x 7	**68.** \$431.29 x 2
69. \$112.98 x 3	**70.** \$201.74 x 4	**71.** \$320.65 x 2	**72.** \$101.72 x 5
73. \$205.97 x 2	**74.** \$118.83 x 5	**75.** \$316.75 x 3	**76.** \$409.68 x 2

F Read each problem carefully. Solve it on a separate sheet of paper. Write your answer on the line beside each problem.

77. Lisa's pay is \$283.85 per week. How much money does she earn in 4 weeks? __________

78. Joe's mortgage payment is \$576.25 per month. How much does he pay in 6 months? __________

Multiplication—Double Multipliers, Part 1

Lesson 14

UNIT 2

In these problems, you will multiply money by whole numbers. Each problem has a dollar sign and a decimal point. The product must also have a dollar sign and a decimal point. Since there are two decimal places in the multiplicand, count two decimal places in the product.

A Multiply.

1. \$.12 x 20	**2.** \$.23 x 13	**3.** \$.41 x 21	**4.** \$.55 x 11
5. \$.28 x 13	**6.** \$.18 x 15	**7.** \$.23 x 24	**8.** \$.12 x 36
9. \$.35 x 46	**10.** \$.58 x 53	**11.** \$.67 x 34	**12.** \$.79 x 22
13. \$.24 x 20	**14.** \$.46 x 10	**15.** \$.80 x 10	**16.** \$.33 x 30

B Use a calculator to solve the following problems.

17. \$.18 x 25	**18.** \$.19 x 30	**19.** \$.65 x 10	**20.** \$.45 x 20
21. \$.69 x 15	**22.** \$.27 x 10	**23.** \$.38 x 14	**24.** \$.44 x 11

UNIT 2

Multiplication—Double Multipliers, Part 2

 Multiply. Check your work.

25. $1.42 x 27

26. $3.75 x 15

27. $5.67 x 44

28. $3.69 x 47

29. $2.37 x 43

30. $9.08 x 26

31. $5.06 x 38

32. $8.19 x 55

33. $9.18 x 34

34. $2.99 x 33

35. $6.97 x 63

36. $4.39 x 28

37. $7.86 x 28

38. $7.04 x 56

39. $9.78 x 29

40. $6.48 x 70

D Read each problem carefully. Solve it on a separate sheet of paper. Write your answer on the line beside each problem.

41. Bruno's weekly salary is $615.86. A quarter of a year is 13 weeks. How much will Bruno earn in one quarter of a year? ______________

42. Mr. Crosley pays Richard $5.15 to work in his sandwich shop. Richard works from 10:30 in the morning until 6:30 at night. How much does he earn in one day? ______________

Multiplication Practice

Lesson 15

Each problem has a dollar sign and a decimal point. Since there are two decimal places in the multiplicand, count two decimal places in the product.

A Multiply.

1. $.30 x 2	**2.** $.15 x 5	**3.** $.28 x 3	**4.** $.85 x 6	**5.** $.71 x 8	**6.** $.98 x 9
7. $3.02 x 3	**8.** $1.09 x 7	**9.** $1.48 x 4	**10.** $7.98 x 8	**11.** $8.50 x 6	**12.** $6.07 x 9
13. $21.15 x 4	**14.** $32.49 x 2	**15.** $11.19 x 5	**16.** $48.96 x 7	**17.** $83.19 x 8	**18.** $64.39 x 6

B Read each problem carefully. Solve it on a separate sheet of paper. Write your answer on the line beside each problem.

19. Aletha sells her chocolate chip cookies for $.79 a piece. How much do 94 cookies cost? ________________

20. Andrew's customer has chosen wallpaper that costs $7.86 per roll. How much will 10 rolls cost? ________________

Multiplication Practice—Double Multipliers

Each problem has a dollar sign and a decimal point. Since there are two decimal places in the multiplicand, count two decimal places in the product.

 Multiply.

1. \$24.80 x 14	2. \$19.81 x 29	3. \$10.46 x 87	4. \$11.99 x 44
5. \$36.24 x 37	6. \$28.56 x 64	7. \$32.06 x 38	8. \$44.10 x 60
9. \$47.47 x 74	10. \$38.09 x 82	11. \$46.92 x 52	12. \$91.43 x 28
13. \$78.07 x 56	14. \$52.19 x 39	15. \$60.60 x 40	16. \$94.26 x 96

Dividing Change

Lesson 17

UNIT 2

These problems have dollar signs and decimal points. To correctly solve each problem, the dollar sign and the decimal point must be placed in the quotient. Decimal points in the quotients must be placed above the decimal points in the problems. Study the example and complete the problems.

Example:

$$\begin{array}{rl} & \$\ .03 \leftarrow \text{quotient} \\ \text{divisor} \rightarrow 3 & \overline{)\$\ .09} \leftarrow \text{dividend} \\ & \underline{-\ 09} \\ & \quad\ 0 \end{array}$$

 Divide.

1. $2\overline{)\$.08}$
2. $4\overline{)\$.12}$
3. $9\overline{)\$.09}$
4. $2\overline{)\$.04}$
5. $4\overline{)\$.16}$
6. $8\overline{)\$.64}$
7. $5\overline{)\$.30}$
8. $9\overline{)\$.72}$
9. $2\overline{)\$.82}$
10. $3\overline{)\$.36}$
11. $8\overline{)\$.80}$
12. $4\overline{)\$.48}$
13. $3\overline{)\$.42}$
14. $5\overline{)\$.85}$
15. $6\overline{)\$.72}$
16. $7\overline{)\$.98}$

B Use a calculator to solve the following problems.

17. $2\overline{)\$8.20}$
18. $3\overline{)\$9.93}$
19. $4\overline{)\$4.80}$
20. $6\overline{)\$6.06}$
21. $3\overline{)\$.06}$
22. $7\overline{)\$.49}$
23. $3\overline{)\$.96}$
24. $4\overline{)\$.68}$

Dividing Money—Single Divisors, Part 1

The following exercises have dollar signs and decimal points. To correctly solve each exercise, the dollar sign and the decimal point must be placed in the answer. Decimal points in the answers must be placed above the decimal points in the problems.

Divide.

1. $2\overline{)\$2.48}$
2. $4\overline{)\$8.04}$
3. $2\overline{)\$6.48}$
4. $3\overline{)\$9.30}$
5. $2\overline{)\$8.06}$
6. $3\overline{)\$8.40}$
7. $5\overline{)\$7.05}$
8. $4\overline{)\$9.68}$
9. $6\overline{)\$9.18}$
10. $7\overline{)\$8.96}$
11. $2\overline{)\$3.50}$
12. $4\overline{)\$5.32}$
13. $3\overline{)\$4.71}$
14. $7\overline{)\$8.12}$
15. $5\overline{)\$9.25}$

B Read each problem carefully. Solve it on a separate sheet of paper. Write your answer on the line beside each problem.

16. The restaurant bill is $8.58. If Rob, William, and Tina each pay an equal amount, how much should each person pay? ____________
17. Four tubes of toothpaste cost $8.92. How much does each tube cost? ____________
18. Terry purchased six tablets for $14.94. How much does each tablet cost? ____________

Dividing Money—Single Divisors, Part 2

When you divide, be sure that the decimal points in the answers are placed above the decimal points in the problems.

 Divide.

19. 3)$63.30 **20.** 2)$46.82 **21.** 4)$80.64 **22.** 3)$96.30

23. 2)$36.84 **24.** 4)$56.80 **25.** 3)$72.96 **26.** 2)$50.48

27. 3)$47.16 **28.** 2)$57.90 **29.** 4)$59.08 **30.** 6)$85.80

D Use a calculator to solve the following problems.

31. 4)$67.56 **32.** 3)$82.74 **33.** 5)$78.60 **34.** 4)$90.24

35. 5)$31.20 **36.** 6)$20.52 **37.** 2)$13.70 **38.** 2)$30.48

UNIT 2

Dividing Money—Single Divisors, Part 3

When you divide, be sure that the decimal points in the answers are placed above the decimal points in the problems.

E Divide.

39. $2\overline{)\$642.80}$ **40.** $3\overline{)\$936.03}$ **41.** $4\overline{)\$480.48}$ **42.** $2\overline{)\$864.28}$

43. $3\overline{)\$456.30}$ **44.** $4\overline{)\$564.84}$ **45.** $5\overline{)\$755.50}$ **46.** $2\overline{)\$968.42}$

47. $4\overline{)\$512.84}$ **48.** $3\overline{)\$732.60}$ **49.** $2\overline{)\$790.84}$ **50.** $6\overline{)\$852.60}$

F Solve each problem. Write your answer on the line beside each problem.

51. Jackson's car payment was $791.88 for two months. How much is the payment each month? ____________

52. Sandra spent $377.00 for five hotel rooms for her employees. How much was each room? ____________

Dividing Money—Double Divisors, Part 1

When you divide, be sure that the decimal points in the answers are placed above the decimal points in the problems.

A Divide.

1. 25)$.75
2. 15)$.30
3. 14)$.56
4. 20)$.80
5. 10)$7.60
6. 16)$3.20
7. 25)$7.75
8. 13)$4.55
9. 12)$38.76
10. 18)$58.86
11. 10)$98.60
12. 24)$49.92

B Use a calculator to solve the following problems.

13. 14)$343.00
14. 18)$693.00
15. 26)$507.00
16. 45)$702.00
17. 22)$352.00
18. 17)$408.00
19. 13)$338.00
20. 23)$437.00

Dividing Money—Double Divisors, Part 2

 Divide.

21. $12\overline{)\$3.48}$
22. $26\overline{)\$9.88}$
23. $37\overline{)\$18.87}$
24. $35\overline{)\$8.05}$
25. $49\overline{)\$25.48}$
26. $24\overline{)\$28.56}$
27. $16\overline{)\$15.84}$
28. $38\overline{)\$14.44}$
29. $14\overline{)\$28.70}$
30. $56\overline{)\$98.00}$
31. $40\overline{)\$100.00}$
32. $26\overline{)\$130.52}$
33. $29\overline{)\$87.29}$
34. $45\overline{)\$90.90}$
35. $16\overline{)\$256.00}$
36. $39\overline{)\$44.07}$

D Read each problem carefully. Solve it on a separate sheet of paper. Write your answer on the line beside each problem.

37. Sophie's tour group had $90.24 in its lunch allowance for a trip to the state capital. There are 12 people in the tour group. How much will each group member be able to spend on lunch? ____________

38. Jesse bought 14 books for $55.30 at the library's annual sale. About how much did he spend on each book? ____________

Division—Horizontal

Lesson 20

UNIT 2

A division problem is sometimes written horizontally (side by side). Rewrite the problem to find the quotient. To correctly solve each problem, you must place the dollar sign in the answer. The decimal point in the quotient must be placed above the decimal point in the problem. Study the example.

Example:

```
                                    $286.57 ← Quotient
$859.71 ÷ 3 = $286.57   Divisor → 3)$859.71 ← Dividend
                                   -6
                                    25
                                   -24
                                     19
                                    -18        Check:
                                      17          $286.57 ← Quotient
                                     -15          x     3 ← Divisor
                                       21         $859.71 ← Dividend
                                      -21
                                        0
```

Rewrite each problem. Divide. Then check each answer.

1. $3.96 ÷ 3 = ________

2. $7.60 ÷ 5 = ________

3. $2.94 ÷ 6 = ________

4. $71.52 ÷ 3 = ________

5. $39.40 ÷ 4 = ________

6. $826.74 ÷ 3 = ________

UNIT 2

Division Practice

A Divide. Then check each answer. The decimal point in the quotient must be placed directly above the decimal point in the problem.

1. 5)$9.63
2. 2)$6.92
3. 5)$9.00
4. 8)$9.84
5. 6)$8.70
6. 5)$74.85
7. 2)$69.78
8. 8)$67.92
9. 9)$48.78
10. 4)$62.08
11. 7)$597.94
12. 4)$359.00
13. 6)$989.76
14. 5)$282.00
15. 9)$788.76

B Use a calculator to solve the following problems.

16. 14)$74.06
17. 26)$97.50
18. 34)$89.42
19. 53)$78.97
20. 17)$97.58
21. 18)$765.00
22. 35)$938.00
23. 26)$819.00
24. 65)$949.00
25. 15)$954.00

Review of Decimal Points

Answer each of the following questions.

1. Why is the decimal point an important symbol in writing amounts of money?

____

2. Where is the dollar sign placed in writing amounts of money?

____

3. Read the following amounts of money: $9.76 and $976.

   a. Which amount has dollars and cents? ____________

   b. Which amount has dollars only? ____________

   c. Which amount is worth more money? ____________ Why?

   ____

4. Where should a decimal point be placed in the answers of addition and subtraction problems?

____

5. Where should a decimal point be placed in the answer of a multiplication problem?

____

6. Where should a decimal point be placed in the answer of a division problem?

____

7. Write out the following amounts of money in numerals.

   a. Two dollars and fifty cents ____________

   b. Two hundred fifty dollars ____________

   c. Five hundred ten dollars ____________

   d. Five dollars and ten cents ____________

   e. Eight dollars and twenty-five cents ____________

   f. Eight hundred twenty-five dollars ____________

   g. One hundred five dollars ____________

   h. One dollar and five cents ____________

   i. Seventy-two cents ____________

   j. Seven dollars and two cents ____________

   k. Seventy-two dollars ____________

   l. Seven hundred two dollars ____________

R E V I E W

Review: Unit 2

A Add. Decimal points must be lined up one under the other.

1.	2.	3.	4.	5.
\$41.26	\$32.86	\$58.75	\$126.47	\$570.35
10.54	18.95	25.18	233.56	199.08
+ 7.25	+ 10.86	+ 35.24	+ 80.15	+ 631.82

B Subtract. Then check your answer. Decimal points must be lined up one under the other.

6.	7.	8.	9.	10.
\$463.50	\$785.42	\$521.35	\$764.25	\$900.00
– 230.45	– 140.56	– 113.96	– 35.87	– 345.72

C Multiply. Then check your answer.

11.	12.	13.	14.	15.	16.
\$2.01	\$1.08	\$1.35	\$8.67	\$6.80	\$7.09
x 4	x 9	x 5	x 8	x 5	x 7

17.	18.	19.	20.	21.	22.
\$8.76	\$2.31	\$3.02	\$1.19	\$4.06	\$9.87
x 10	x 34	x 23	x 57	x 48	x 86

D Divide. Then check each answer.

23.	24.	25.	26.	27.
2)\$8.60	3)\$9.84	5)\$7.00	4)\$59.04	9)\$68.31

28.	29.	30.	31.	32.
18)\$675.00	36)\$963.00	24)\$420.00	15)\$864.00	62)\$775.00

Introduction to Counting Money

Introduction to Counting Money
Counting money is an important skill. This chapter will give you practice in counting money.

Howard Williams is treasurer of his community theater group. He is counting money from the sale of tickets to the annual play. Howard is using the chart below to keep a record of the money he collected. He collected ten of each denomination of coins and bills.

A Finish the chart that Howard started.

	1	2	3	4	5	6	7	8	9	10
Pennies	$.01	$.02	$.03	$.04	$.05	$.06				
Nickels	$.05	$.10	$.15	$.20						
Dimes	$.10	$.20	$.30							
Quarters	$.25	$.50	$.75							
Half-dollar Bills	$.50	$1.00	$1.50							
One-dollars Bills	$1.00	$2.00	$3.00							
Five-dollars Bills	$5.00	$10.00	$15.00							
Ten-dollars Bills	$10.00	$20.00	$30.00							

B Help Howard add up the total money taken in from the sale of the tickets.

Pennies ______________________

Nickels ______________________

Dimes ______________________

Quarters ______________________

Half-dollars ______________________

One-dollar Bills ______________________

Five-dollar Bills ______________________

Ten-dollar Bills ______________________

Total ______________________

UNIT 3

Counting Chart—To $10

Kim Romanoff is counting the money made from the sale of tickets for a field trip to the state historical museum. Kim is using the chart below to keep a record of the money she collected today.

A Finish the chart that Kim started.

	1	2	3	4	5	6	7	8	9
Pennies	$.01	$.02	$.03						
Nickels	$.05	$.10							
Dimes	$.10								
Quarters	$.25	$.50							
Half-dollars	$.50								
One-dollar Bills	$1.00	$2.00							
Five-dollar Bills	$5.00								
Ten-dollar Bills	$10.00	$20.00							

B Help Kim add up the money from today's ticket sales.

Pennies ______________________________

Nickels ______________________________

Dimes ______________________________

Quarters ______________________________

Half-dollars ______________________________

One-dollar Bills ______________________________

Five-dollar Bills ______________________________

Ten-dollar Bills ______________________________

Total ______________________________

Counting Chart—To $20

Teresa Gomez is using the chart below to keep a record of the money that was collected for travel club dues.

A Finish the chart that Teresa started.

	1	2	3	4	5	6	7	8	9
Pennies	$.01	$.02	$.03	$.04					
Nickels	$.05	$.10	$.15						
Dimes	$.10	$.20	$.30						
Quarters	$.25	$.50	$.75						
Half-dollars	$.50	$1.00	$1.50						
One-dollar Bills	$1.00	$2.00	$3.00						
Five-dollar Bills	$5.00	$10.00							
Ten-dollar Bills	$10.00	$20.00							
Twenty-dollar Bills	$20.00	$40.00							

B What is the total that Teresa collected for club dues?

Pennies ______________________

Nickels ______________________

Dimes ______________________

Quarters ______________________

Half-dollars ______________________

One-dollar Bills ______________________

Five-dollar Bills______________________

Ten-dollar Bills ______________________

Twenty-dollar Bills ______________________

Total ______________________

U N I T 3

Complete the Chart

Howard Wing is using the chart to count the money that was collected from the sale of tickets for the hayride and barbecue.

A Finish the chart that Howard started.

	1	2	3	4	5	6	7	8	9
Pennies	$.01	$.02	$.03	$.04					
Nickels	$.05	$.10	$.15						
Dimes	$.10	$.20	$.30						
Quarters	$.25	$.50	$.75						
Half-dollars	$.50	$1.00	$1.50						
One-dollar Bills	$1.00	$2.00	$3.00						
Five-dollar Bills	$5.00	$10.00	$15.00						
Ten-dollar Bills	$10.00	$20.00	$30.00						
Twenty-dollar Bills	$20.00	$40.00							

B Help Howard compute the total money collected for ticket sales.

Pennies ____________________

Nickels ____________________

Dimes ____________________

Quarters ____________________

Half-dollars ____________________

One-dollar Bills ____________________

Five-dollar Bills ____________________

Ten-dollar Bills ____________________

Twenty-dollar Bills ____________________

Total ____________________

Money Chart—To $50

James is using the chart below to record the money he collected for tickets to his community band concert.

A Finish the chart that James started.

	1	2	3	4	5	6	7	8	9
Pennies	$.01	$.02	$.03	$.04	$.05				
Nickels	$.05	$.10	$.15	$.20	$.25				
Dimes	$.10	$.20	$.30	$.40					
Quarters	$.25	$.50	$.75	$1.00					
Half-dollars	$.50	$1.00	$1.50						
One-dollar Bills	$1.00	$2.00	$3.00						
Five-dollar Bills	$5.00	$10.00	$15.00						
Ten-dollar Bills	$10.00	$20.00							
Twenty-dollar Bills	$20.00	$40.00							
Fifty-dollar Bills	$50.00	$100.00							

B What is the total that James collected for concert tickets?

Pennies ____________________

Nickels ____________________

Dimes ____________________

Quarters ____________________

Half-dollars ____________________

One-dollar Bills ____________________

Five-dollar Bills ____________________

Ten-dollar Bills ____________________

Twenty-dollar Bills ____________________

Fifty-dollar Bills ____________________

Total ____________________

UNIT 3

Count the Money, Part 1

A Sheila had $22.50 in her cash drawer when she started her shift at the hardware store. She then collected the following amounts of coins and paper currency. What was the total amount of money she collected?

35 pennies	$.35
14 nickels	______
22 dimes	______
12 quarters	______
8 half-dollars	______
24 one-dollar bills	______
7 five-dollar bills	______
3 ten-dollar bills	______
2 twenty-dollar bills	______
Total	______

B Tom collected the following amounts of coins and paper currency on his shift at the hardware store. What was the total amount of money he collected?

72 pennies	______
12 nickels	______
9 dimes	______
7 quarters	______
5 half-dollars	______
9 one-dollar bills	______
2 ten-dollar bills	______
3 twenty-dollar bills	______
1 fifty-dollar bill	______
Total	______

What was the total amount of money collected by Sheila and Tom? ______

Count the Money, Part 2

C Maria had $125.00. She wanted to save enough money to buy a video camera. She added the following amounts of coins and currency to the money she already had. Determine the total amount of money Maria saved.

24 pennies ____________________

25 nickels ____________________

16 dimes ____________________

22 quarters ____________________

11 half-dollars ____________________

18 one-dollar bills ____________________

10 five-dollar bills ____________________

3 ten-dollar bills ____________________

4 twenty-dollar bills ____________________

Total ____________________

Maria bought a video camera for $173.50. How much money did she have left? ____________________

D At the street fair, Josh tried to guess the amount of money in five jars of coins and one jar of ten-dollar bills. How much money did each jar contain?

316 pennies ____________________

292 nickels ____________________

387 dimes ____________________

264 quarters ____________________

197 half-dollars ____________________

43 ten-dollar bills ____________________

What was the total amount of money in the jars? ____________________

Count the Money, Part 3

E Tina counted the following amounts of coins and paper currency in her bakery's cash register on Wednesday. What was the total amount of coins and currency in the cash register?

98 pennies	____________
16 nickels	____________
13 dimes	____________
16 quarters	____________
10 half-dollars	____________
12 one-dollar bills	____________
10 five-dollar bills	____________
3 ten-dollar bills	____________
3 twenty-dollar bills	____________
Total	____________

In addition, Tina had checks for the following amounts: $20.00, $10.00, and $12.74. What was the total amount of money in the cash register on Wednesday? ____________

On Tuesday, Tina had a total of $208.74 in the cash register. How much more did she have on Tuesday than on Wednesday? ____________

F On Friday, Tina made a deposit at the bank. The deposit included the coins, currency, and checks below. What was the total amount of the deposit?

457 pennies	____________
96 nickels	____________
84 dimes	____________
86 quarters	____________
31 half-dollars	____________
120 one-dollar bills	____________
51 ten-dollar bills	____________
22 twenty-dollar bills	____________
Checks	$37.00
Total	____________

Find the Total Amounts

Read the problems and answer the question.

On Thursday, William received the following amounts of coins and paper currency in his shop. What was the total amount of money he received?

106 pennies	__________
17 nickels	__________
25 dimes	__________
8 quarters	__________
6 half-dollars	__________
28 one-dollar bills	__________
13 five-dollar bills	__________
2 ten-dollar bills	__________
Total	__________

On Friday, William received the following amounts of coins and paper currency in his shop. What was the total amount of money he received?

23 pennies	__________
12 nickels	__________
19 dimes	__________
10 quarters	__________
9 half-dollars	__________
35 one-dollar bills	__________
9 ten-dollar bills	__________
3 twenty-dollar bills	__________
Total	__________

What was the total amount of money William received in his shop on Thursday and Friday? __________

How much more money did William receive on Friday than on Thursday? __________

Total Amounts of Money

Read the problems and answer the questions.

In April, Julio saved the following amounts of coins and paper currency. How much money did he save in April?

34 pennies ____________

42 nickels ____________

31 dimes ____________

10 quarters ____________

5 half-dollars ____________

24 one-dollar bills ____________

9 five-dollar bills ____________

1 ten-dollar bill ____________

Total ____________

In May, Julio saved the following amounts of coins and paper currency. How much money did he save in May?

57 pennies ____________

81 nickels ____________

20 dimes ____________

9 quarters ____________

6 half-dollars ____________

31 one-dollar bills ____________

8 five-dollar bills ____________

3 ten-dollar bills ____________

Total ____________

What was the total amount of money Julio saved in April and May? ____________

How much more money did Julio save in May than in April? ____________

Review: Unit 3

REVIEW

A Sandra is using the chart below to count the money received during the week in her quilt shop. Finish the chart.

	1	2	3	4	5	6	7	8	9
Pennies	$.01	$.02	$.03	$.04					
Nickels	$.05	$.10	$.15	$.20					
Dimes	$.10	$.20	$.30						
Quarters	$.25	$.50	$.75						
Half-dollars	$.50	$1.00	$1.50						
One-dollar Bills	$1.00	$2.00	$3.00						
Five-dollar Bills	$5.00	$10.00	$15.00						
Ten-dollar Bills	$10.00	$20.00							
Twenty-dollar Bills	$20.00	$40.00							
Fifty-dollar Bills	$50.00	$100.00							

What was the total amount of money that Sandra received for the week? ______________

B Read the problem and answer the question. The next week, the cash drawer at Sandra's quilt shop contained the following amounts of coins and paper currency.

42 pennies ______________

29 nickels ______________

54 dimes ______________

36 quarters ______________

3 half-dollars ______________

34 one-dollar bills ______________

12 five-dollar bills ______________

9 ten-dollar bills ______________

6 twenty-dollar bills ______________

Total ______________

How much more money did the quilt shop make during the first week? ______________

REVIEW

C Read the problems and answer the questions.

Antoinette received the following amounts of coins and paper currency for tips during her shift at the restaurant on Saturday night. What was the total amount she received?

116 pennies	______
13 nickels	______
30 dimes	______
9 quarters	______
7 half-dollars	______
17 one-dollar bills	______
12 five-dollar bills	______
4 ten-dollar bills	______
Total	______

Sharon received the following amounts of coins and paper currency for tips during her shift at the restaurant on Saturday night. What was the total amount she received?

35 pennies	______
17 nickels	______
23 dimes	______
7 quarters	______
5 half-dollars	______
26 one-dollar bills	______
16 five-dollar bills	______
5 ten-dollar bills	______
Total	______

What was the total amount of tips Antoinette and Sharon received on Saturday night? ______

How much more money did Sharon make than Antoinette? ______

Addition Problems

This chapter will give you practice solving word problems that involve money.

When you solve a word problem, first read the problem carefully. Then write the problem in numeral form and solve it.

Write each addition word problem below in numeral form. Then find the solution.

1. Markelos bought two books on sale. One cost $4.49 and the other cost $8.48. How much did Markelos spend on the books?

   ______
   + ______
   Total ______

2. At the hardware store, Olga bought a can of paint for $19.95, a brush for $4.45, and a ladder for $84.60. How much did she spend in all?

   ______
   ______
   + ______
   Total ______

3. Sam earned $67.50 one week. He earned $73.00 the next. He earned $35.00 the next. How much did he earn for the three weeks?

   ______
   ______
   + ______
   Total ______

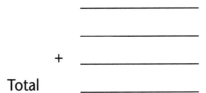

4. Jeanette bought a shirt for $39.50, a sweater for $45.50, and a pair of jeans for $28.99. What was the total amount she spent for clothes?

   ______
   ______
   + ______
   Total ______

UNIT 4

Solving Addition Problems

Read each problem carefully. Solve it on a separate sheet of paper. Write your answer on the line beside each problem.

1. Anna spent $15.50 for child care on Monday, $22.50 on Tuesday, and $21.00 on Wednesday. How much did she spend on child care for these three days? ____________

2. Monique bought a can of coffee for $4.29, a case of soft drinks for $7.57, and a steak for $5.96. How much did she spend in all? ____________

3. At the amusement park, Jeremy spent $19.50 for admission, $18.00 for rides, and $19.21 for food. How much did he spend in all? ____________

4. Patrick's telephone bill was $26.42 for June, $25.84 for July, and $24.13 for August. What was the total of the bills for the three months? ____________

5. Rosa paid $22.50 for a poster, $51.95 for a lamp, and $19.12 for a vase. How much did she spend in all? ____________

6. Lu Ann bought a rug for $138.00, a chair for $157.00, and a desk for $85.00. How much did she spend in all? ____________

7. The community theater group spent $84.75 on costumes and $52.51 on props. How much did the group spend for these items? ____________

8. Raoul earned $264.86 at his part-time job one week, $287.94 the next, and $314.10 the next. What were his total earnings for the three weeks? ____________

9. On Saturday, Lance spent $42.76 at the supermarket, $27.85 at the drugstore, and $14.27 at the gas station. How much did he spend? ____________

10. Tim bought a suit for $475.00, a shirt for $49.95, and a tie for $27.76. How much did he spend? ____________

Subtraction

Read each problem carefully. Solve it on a separate sheet of paper. Write your answer on the line beside each problem.

1. Linda bought a set of paints for $7.98. How much change would she receive if she gave the cashier a $20.00 bill? ____________

2. Tony made $164.50 per week as a lifeguard. He makes $180.50 per week as a computer operator. How much more money does he make each week as a computer operator? ____________

3. Candace had $22.07. She bought a CD for $14.95. How much money did she have left? ____________

4. Alex's grocery bill was $48.43. He gave the cashier a $100.00 bill. How much change should he have received? ____________

5. Terence has saved $204.44. He wants to buy a VCR that costs $249.99. How much more money does he need? ____________

6. Julia had $688.63 in her checking account. She has written checks totaling $501.63. How much money is left in her account? ____________

7. The Chongs spent $767.15 on groceries in May. They spent $951.78 on groceries in June. How much more did they spend on groceries in June than in May? ____________

8. Ben had $937.85 in his savings account. He withdrew $455.10. How much was left in his account? ____________

9. Imran wants to buy a camera. Camera A costs $248.98. Camera B costs $160.62. How much more expensive is camera A than camera B? ____________

10. James borrowed $250.00 from his sister on April 1. On April 15, he paid back $168.75. How much did James still owe? ____________

Subtraction Money Problems

Read each problem carefully. Solve it on a separate sheet of paper. Write your answer on the line beside each problem.

1. Belinda bought a sweater for $25.74. How much change should she receive from a $50.00 bill? __________

2. James spent $63.95 for two paintings. One cost $36.95. How much did the other one cost? __________

3. Mahmoud had $62.17 in his wallet before he went shopping. When he returned from the mall he had $36.95. How much did he spend at the mall? __________

4. The dinner bill for the Orlandos and the Levins was $73.19. The Orlandos' share was $42.91. How much was the Levins' share? __________

5. Yolanda's paycheck for one week was $248.73. After paying for child care, she had $184.41. How much did she pay for child care? __________

6. Luis bought a shirt and a jacket for $120.95. The shirt cost $36.95. How much was the jacket? __________

7. Deedee brings home earnings of $1,705.00 per month. If she pays $545.00 for rent each month, how much money will she have left? __________

8. A plane ticket from New York to Miami costs $318.50 on airline A. It costs $407.00 on airline B. How much more does the ticket cost on airline B? __________

9. An Li had $852.25 in her checking account. After paying a bill, she had $760.33. How much was the bill? __________

10. Leslie's savings account had a balance of $827.14. She transferred $168.73 to her checking account. What was the new balance in her savings account? __________

Addition and Subtraction

Read each problem carefully. Solve it on a separate sheet of paper. Write your answer on the line beside each problem.

1. Lu and Sarah went to a department store. Lu spent $88.39. Sarah spent $51.13. What was the total amount that Lu and Sarah spent? ____________

2. On Monday Mrs. Wong spent $74.94 for groceries. On Friday she spent $52.82. How much more did she spend on Monday than on Friday? ____________

3. Last year Stefka spent $97.56 on birthday gifts. This year she spent $178.99. How much more did she spend this year than last year? ____________

4. William spent $430.50 on stereo equipment. Raoul spent $355.46. How much more did William spend than Raoul? ____________

5. Michael made $126.75 mowing lawns last week. He made $95.87 this week. What were his total earnings for two weeks? ____________

6. In January, Rosa put $467.32 in her savings account. In February, she put $290.74 in the account. How much more did she deposit in January than in February? ____________

7. Juan and Sharon bought a table for $325.97, a chair for $122.49, and a chest of drawers for $386.18. What was the total amount they spent for the three pieces of furniture? ____________

8. Eve had $443.57 in her checking account. She wrote a check for $392.32. How much was left in her account? ____________

9. On her trip to Florida, Whitney's restaurant meals for three days were $36.29, $44.64, and $42.57. What was the total amount she spent for meals for three days? ____________

10. Jessica opened a checking account with deposits of $255.80 and $329.10. Then she wrote a check for $117.42. How much was left in her account? ____________

More Addition and Subtraction

Read each problem carefully. Solve it on a separate sheet of paper. Write your answer on the line beside each problem.

1. Eddie saw two cameras that he liked. One cost $90.78. The other cost $72.20. What was the difference in price between the cameras? ________________

2. Ellen paid two telephone bills. One was $73.37. The other was $85.99. What was the total of the two bills? ________________

3. The Kims' heating bill for January was $96.02. Their heating bill in March was $57.90. How much higher was the January heating bill? ________________

4. Yvette made three sales during her shift at the gift shop. One was $65.07, one was $81.19, and the third was $38.70. What was the total amount of Yvette's sales? ________________

5. Jesse had $333.47 in his checking account. After he wrote a check for groceries, he had $265.54. How much did he spend for groceries? ________________

6. Teresa had $794.42 in her college savings fund. She added a check from her grandmother for $130.00. What was the total amount in the fund? ________________

7. Jackie paid three bills for her accounting firm. They were for $47.80, $217.62, and $100.99. What was the total amount of the bills? ________________

8. Andrew had $786.76 in his checking account. He added his paycheck of $379.81 and a birthday check for $90.00. What was the total amount of money in his account? ________________

9. In September Julio paid bills totaling $823.10. In October he paid bills totaling $693.89. How much more money did he pay in September? ________________

10. Gabriella has $1,043.15 in her savings account, $697.83 in her checking account, and cash on hand of $75.84. How much money does she have? ________________

The Total Price of Products

The symbol @ shows how much one item costs. For example, gasoline @$1.15 means that each gallon of gasoline costs $1.15. To find the total price of two gallons of gasoline, multiply the number of gallons by the price per gallon: 2 x $1.15 = $2.30.

Read each problem carefully. Solve it on a separate sheet of paper. Write your answer on the line beside each problem.

1. Rita bought 4 cans of soup @ $.85. How much did she spend? ______________
2. Joe bought 8 boxes of crackers @ $.99. How much did he spend? ______________
3. Jess bought 3 pens @ $2.29. How much did he spend? ______________
4. Pia bought 5 plants @ $1.59. How much did she spend? ______________
5. Matt bought 8 gallons of milk @ $1.94. How much did he spend? ______________
6. Marisa bought 8 cans of cat food @ $.79 and 6 cans of cat food @ $1.61. How much did she spend? ______________
7. Peter bought 12 folders @ $1.19 and 6 notebooks @ $2.61. How much did he spend? ______________
8. Alicia bought 9 cans of fruit @ $.96 and 8 boxes of noodles @ $1.67. How much did she spend? ______________
9. Carlos bought 14 jars of baby food @ $.89 and 5 gallons of ice cream @ $5.50. How much did he spend? ______________
10. Gia bought 9 napkins @ $.69 and 6 placemats @ $1.95. How much did she spend? ______________
11. Jade bought 5 drawing pads @ $4.99. How much did she spend? ______________
12. Toni bought 7 rolls of wallpaper @ $15.70. How much did she spend? ______________

Find the Total Price

Read each problem carefully. Solve it on a separate sheet of paper. Write your answer on the line beside each problem.

1. Lucy bought 4 cans of corn @ $.79. How much did she spend? __________

2. Pat bought 8 bars of soap @ $.55. How much did she spend? __________

3. Justin bought 9 grapefruit @ $.59. How much did he spend? __________

4. Roseanna bought 5 boxes of tissues @ $1.49. How much did she spend? __________

5. Jorge bought 16 notepads @ $1.22. How much did he spend? __________

6. Bill bought 5 sacks of apples @ $3.58. How much did he spend? __________

7. Chris bought 8 sheets of poster board @ $1.29 and 5 sets of markers @ $3.93. How much did he spend? __________

8. Su Li bought 4 pounds of fish @ $7.75. How much did she spend? __________

9. Audrey bought 10 toothbrushes @ $1.79 and 8 tubes of suntan lotion @ $2.50. How much did she spend? __________

10. Noah bought 8 boxes of nails @ $1.79. How much did he spend? __________

11. Marcia bought 12 books @ $2.98 and 20 books @ $2.20. How much did she spend? __________

12. Alex bought 9 loaves of bread @ $1.79 and 8 packs of deli meats @ $2.98. How much did he spend? __________

Multiplication

Read each problem carefully. Solve it on a separate sheet of paper. Write your answer on the line beside each problem.

1. Althea earns $5.87 per hour. How much money would she earn if she worked

   5 hours? ________ 9 hours? ________ 20 hours? ________

2. A ticket for the circus costs $13.75. What is the cost of

   3 tickets? ________ 5 tickets? ________ 14 tickets? ________

3. One paperback book costs $4.75. What is the cost of

   4 books? ________ 7 books? ________ 12 books? ________

4. Dr. Nichols charges $15.00 for an X ray. What would be the charge for

   3 X rays? ________ 6 X rays? ________ 12 X rays? ________

5. Ben bought 6 CDs. Each CD cost $12.99. What was the total cost of the CDs? ________

6. Angela pays her babysitter $4.50 per hour. How much would she pay her for 3 hours? ________

7. Dan spends $2.69 for lunch each day. How much would he spend in 4 days? ________

8. The telephone bill for Lee's company is $203.20 per month. How much will the bills total for five months? ________

9. Albert's mortgage payment is $675.00 each month. What is the total amount for five mortgage payments? ________

10. Jayne bought 5 rosebushes. Each bush cost $12.75. What was the total cost of the rosebushes? ________

UNIT 4

Multiplication Problems

Lesson 10

Read each problem carefully. Solve it on a separate sheet of paper. Write your answer on the line beside each problem.

1. One movie ticket costs $7.50. What is the cost of

   6 tickets? ____________ 20 tickets? ____________ 35 tickets? ____________

2. A concert ticket costs $15.75. What is the cost of

   4 tickets? ____________ 7 tickets? ____________ 15 tickets? ____________

3. Kate spends $2.95 each day for bus fare. How much will she spend in

   3 days? ____________ 5 days? ____________ 10 days? ____________

4. School lunch costs $1.50 per day. What is the cost of lunch for 6 days? ____________

5. Dishwashing liquid costs $1.99. What is the cost of 4 bottles? ____________

6. One exercise videotape costs $24.85. What is the cost of 4 videotapes? ____________

7. Anita earns $6.75 per hour. How much money would she earn if she worked 40 hours? ____________

8. A ticket for a baseball game costs $15.00. What is the cost of 30 tickets? ____________

9. A frozen dinner costs $4.43. How much would 14 frozen dinners cost? ____________

10. Charles spends $1.75 each day on newspapers. How much will he spend on newspapers in 5 days? ____________

Division

Read each problem carefully. Solve it on a separate sheet of paper. Write your answer on the line beside each problem.

1. Debra has $90.00 to spend on 20 souvenirs. How much can she spend on each souvenir? __________

2. Adrian spent $44.85 for lunches for 5 days. What was the average amount he spent each day? __________

3. Paolo spent $52.50 for 3 knit shirts. What was the average price of the shirts? __________

4. Darnell's telephone bills for 6 months totaled $207.90. How much did he pay on the average for his telephone bill each month? __________

5. In 4 weeks, the Jacksons have spent $209.92 for groceries. What is the average amount they spent for groceries each week? __________

6. Alberto can buy 4 pine trees for $153.80. What is the average cost of each tree? __________

7. Jane bought 7 lilac bushes for $243.25. What was the cost of each shrub? __________

8. Marian spent $86.10 on notebooks for her nature class to use. She bought 35 notebooks. How much did each notebook cost? __________

9. Lucy's electricity bill for 25 days was $18.25. What was the average charge for electricity each day? __________

10. Mark had $87.00 to spend on birthday gifts for his 3 sisters. How much could he spend on each gift? __________

Division Problems

Read each problem carefully. Solve it on a separate sheet of paper. Write your answer on the line beside each problem.

1. Juan bought 8 sacks of rice for $36.80. What was the average cost of each sack? ____________

2. May-Lin earned $71.76 for 8 hours' work. How much did she earn per hour? ____________

3. On her 5-day trip to New York City, Kelly spent $87.50 on taxis. On the average, how much did she spend on taxis each day? ____________

4. In one year, Beth spent $869.40 on car repairs. On the average, how much did she spend on repairs each month? ____________

5. In 6 months, Isabel gave $269.40 to charity. On the average, how much did she give to charity each month? ____________

6. Patrick bought 7 lighting fixtures for $117.25. What was the average cost of each fixture? ____________

7. Elliot took a 9-day trip. He spent $268.65 on food. On the average, how much did he spend for food each day? ____________

8. In 12 months, Gina saved $1,338.00. On the average, how much did she save each month? ____________

9. Arturo took a 10-day trip. He spent $355.00 on accommodations. On average, how much did he spend on accommodations each day? ____________

10. In 8 months, Glenn spent $191.84 on CDs. On the average, how much did he spend on CDs each month? ____________

Multiplication and Division

Read each problem carefully. Solve it on a separate sheet of paper. Write your answer on the line beside each problem.

1. Khalad earns $8.56 per hour. How much would he earn if he worked

   5 hours? ___________ 19 hours? ___________ 30 hours? ___________

2. A ticket for a basketball game costs $16.75. What is the cost of

   3 tickets? ___________ 7 tickets? ___________ 16 tickets? ___________

3. In 19 months, Anna earned $2,322.75 in overtime. On average, how much overtime pay did she earn each month? ___________

4. Ted earned $470.00 for 40 hours of work. How much did he earn per hour? ___________

5. Coach Scott bought 25 trophies for the members of her soccer team. Each trophy cost $28.91. What was the total cost of the trophies? ___________

6. Kay paid a house painter $9.65 per hour. How much did she owe for 15 hours of work? ___________

7. In 8 weeks, Juanita spent $380.00 at the produce market. On the average, how much did she spend at the market each week? ___________

8. Ellen bought 5 electric fans for $174.75. What was the average cost of each fan? ___________

9. David earned $416.25 for 37 hours of work. How much did he earn per hour? ___________

10. Mrs. Chang paid a baby-sitter $5.25 per hour. How much did the baby-sitter earn for 9 hours? ___________

More Multiplication and Division

Read each problem carefully. Solve it on a separate sheet of paper. Write your answer on the line beside each problem.

1. Yolanda earned $612.56 for 62 hours of work. How much did she earn per hour? ____________

2. A team bought 28 sweatshirts for $670.60. What was the cost of each sweatshirt? ____________

3. During the summer, Robert took 25 boat rides for $6.50 each. What was the total amount he spent on boat rides? ____________

4. In 14 weeks, Julian saved $681.38. What was the average amount he saved each week? ____________

5. In 8 weeks, Charles spent $479.52 for meals at restaurants. On the average, how much did he spend for restaurant meals each week? ____________

6. Tara earned $7.60 per hour. How much did she earn for 6 hours of work? ____________

7. Brad earns $9.16 per hour. How much money would he earn if he worked

   7 hours? ____________ 20 hours? ____________ 36 hours? ____________

8. Fare to the airport costs $14.50. What is the cost of

   5 fares? ____________ 8 fares? ____________ 15 fares? ____________

9. The rental charge for carpet-cleaning equipment is $5.78 per hour. What is the charge for

   7 hours? ____________ 20 hours? ____________ 36 hours? ____________

10. Christine charges $11.75 per hour for cleaning homes. How much will she earn in

    7 hours? ____________ 20 hours? ____________ 36 hours? ____________

Write the Answer

Read each problem carefully. Solve it on a separate sheet of paper. Write your answer on the line beside each problem.

1. Jeffrey found a desk at store A for $379.89. The same desk cost $330.22 at store B. What was the difference in price? ____________

2. Greg bought a pair of tennis shoes for $59.95, socks for $6.40, and a can of tennis balls for $5.74. How much money did he spend? ____________

3. Mary Kay earns $11.78 per hour. How much money would she earn for 7 hours of work? ____________

4. Anita bought 15 notebooks for $67.35. What was the cost of each notebook? ____________

5. Eva has 7 half-dollars, 15 quarters, 22 dimes, 15 nickels, and 65 pennies. How much money does she have? ____________

6. William earned $21.53 each day for 13 days. What was the total amount he earned? ____________

7. Martina bought 2 bottles of milk @ $1.63 and 6 cartons of yogurt @ $.79. How much money did she spend? ____________

8. Marlon bought groceries at Supermarket A for $74.68. Helena bought the same items at Supermarket B for $68.09. How much more expensive were the items at Supermarket A? ____________

9. Mrs. Iverson bought lunch for the 14 members of the Chess Club at the state tournament. She spent $55.86. What was the average price of the lunches? ____________

10. Petra bought 4 pints of strawberries @ $2.49, 2 pounds of bananas @ $.69, and papayas @ $1.59. How much did she spend on fruit? ____________

U N I T 4

Solve the Money Problems

Read each problem carefully. Solve it on a separate sheet of paper. Write your answer on the line beside each problem.

1. Jan had $972.43 to pay the following bills: rent, $490.50; utilities, $93.18; groceries, $105.28; credit cards, $195.50. How much was the total? How much did she have left?

Step 1

Rent ____________

Utilities ____________

Groceries ____________

Credit cards ____________

Total expenses ____________

Step 2

Money Jan had ____________

Jan's total expenses ____________

Cash on hand (balance) ____________

2. Luz has the following coins: 4 half-dollars; 15 quarters; 28 dimes; 27 nickels; 64 pennies. How much money does she have? ____________

3. Marla earned $84.24 for 12 hours of work. How much did she earn per hour? ____________

4. Anton wants to buy a bicycle that costs $378.50. He has saved $340.72. How much more money does he need? ____________

5. Pedro bought a shirt for $29.50, a sweater for $42.95, a pair of pants for $39.95, and a jacket for $78.60. What was the total amount he spent on clothing? ____________

6. Judith and her 12 friends want to divide their $105.30 bill for lunch evenly. How much should each person pay? ____________

7. Kenneth has 3 half-dollars, 9 quarters, 22 dimes, 18 nickels, and 79 pennies. How much money does he have? ____________

8. Teresa bought 6 lilies @ $3.85, 12 black-eyed susans @ $2.05, and 8 carnations @ $.85. How much did she spend on flowers? ____________

Money Word Problems

Read each problem carefully. Solve it on a separate sheet of paper. Write your answer on the line beside each problem.

1. Mrs. MacDonald had $450.00 before she went shopping. She now has $75.14 left. How much money did she spend? __________

2. Jan has 7 half-dollars, 17 quarters, 31 dimes, 19 nickels, and 57 pennies. How much money does she have? __________

3. Angel saved $155.10 in 6 weeks. On the average, how much money did he save each week? __________

4. Martha saved $30.75 one week, $43.60 the second week, and $27.19 the third week. How much money did she save? __________

5. Mr. Cheng bought 3 cans of motor oil @ $.98 and 2 air filters @ $2.99. How much money did he spend? __________

6. Delores wants to buy an electric typewriter for $417.00. She has $238.45. How much more money does she need? __________

7. Rick paid the following bills: rent—$350.00; utilities—$63.08; food—$73.94; and car repair—$52.75. How much money did he pay? __________

8. Mr. Foster bought 14 gifts for $329.00. On the average, how much money did he pay for each gift? __________

9. John earns $6.08 per hour. How much would he earn if he worked

   8 hours? ________ 7 hours? ________ 30 hours? ________

10. Admission to a theme park costs $13.25. What is the cost of

    5 tickets? ________ 9 tickets? ________ 12 tickets? ________

11. A ticket for a rock concert costs $16.50. What is the cost of

    5 tickets? ________ 7 tickets? ________ 12 tickets? ________

12. Ken earns $5.78 per hour. How much money would he earn if he worked

    6 hours? ________ 8 hours? ________ 30 hours? ________

UNIT 4

Find the Amount of Money

Lesson 18

Read each problem carefully. Solve it on a separate sheet of paper. Write your answer on the line beside each problem.

1. Danny saved $18.35 one week, $51.72 the second week, and $40.50 the third week. How much money did he save in three weeks? ________________

2. Ricardo has 11 half-dollars, 9 quarters, 18 dimes, 35 nickels, and 31 pennies. How much money does he have? ________________

3. Boris wants to buy a 35-mm camera for $289.00. He has $179.75. How much more money does he need to buy it? ________________

4. Ara had $205.00 before he went shopping. He now has $184.75. How much money did he spend? ________________

5. Mrs. Lau spent $632.00 during the past 16 weeks for plumbing repairs. On the average, how much money did she spend each week? ________________

6. Athena has $112.50 to buy 8 gifts. On the average, how much can she spend for each gift? ________________

7. Vicki bought 2 bottles of shampoo @ $3.95 and 3 tubes of toothpaste @ $1.59. How much money did she spend? ________________

8. Keesha went shopping. She spent $24.15 at Food City, $34.85 at SmartMart, and $80.60 at Odd Job. How much money did she spend? ________________

9. Dominic took $100.00 to the fleamarket. He bought an armchair for $58.95 and a set of old records for $13.65. How much money did he have left? ________________

10. Elise has $897.51 in her savings account, $516.37 in her checking account, and $2,115.26 in a business account. What is the total amount of money in her accounts? ________________

11. Annie earns $4.68 per hour. How much would she earn if she worked

    4 hours? __________ 6 hours? __________ 40 hours? __________

12. A ticket for a hockey game costs $15.75. What is the cost of

    3 tickets? __________ 8 tickets? __________ 12 tickets? __________

Solve the Problems

Read each problem carefully. Solve it on a separate sheet of paper. Write your answer on the line beside each problem.

1. The Chabras had $1,203.52 to pay the following bills: mortgage $715.50, utilities—$121.28, groceries—$110.68, and credit cards—$187.92. What was the total? How much was left?

Step 1

Mortgage payment ____________
Utilities ____________
Groceries ____________
Credit cards ____________

Total expenses ____________

Step 2

Money the Chabras had ____________
The Chabras' total expenses ____________
Cash on hand (balance) ____________

2. Alfredo has the following coins: 12 half-dollars; 19 quarters; 2 dimes; 30 nickels; 47 pennies. How much money does he have? ____________________

3. Magda saved $45.90 one month; $109.85 the second month; and $58.35 the third month. How much money did she save? ____________________

4. Lisa has 29 quarters. How much money does she have? ____________________

5. Alex had $260.75 before he went shopping. If he now has $82.90, how much money did he spend? ____________________

6. Mrs. Stein saved $238.00 during the past 5 weeks. On the average, how much money did she save each week? ____________________

7. Mr. Purelku wants to buy a television for $630.00. He has saved $391.75. How much more money does he need to buy the television? ____________________

8. Yolanda spent $539.00 during the past 14 weeks for furnishings for her apartment. On the average, how much money did she spend each week? ____________________

Problems to Solve

Read each problem carefully. Solve it on a separate sheet of paper. Write your answer on the line beside each problem.

1. Tony saved $60.70 one week, $35.00 the second week, and $20.95 the third week. How much money did he save? ______________

2. Janina had $132.00 before she went shopping. She now has $63.07. How much money did she spend? ______________

3. Lewis saved $285.90 during the past 6 months. How much money did he save each month? ______________

4. Alex had $260.75 before he went shopping. If he now has $82.90, how much money did he spend? ______________

5. The drama club spent $474.00 during the past 12 weeks for fabric to make costumes. How much money did it spend each week? ______________

6. Chang wants to buy a personal computer for $835.00. He has saved $489.50. How much more does he need to buy the PC? ______________

7. Carlos has 19 quarters. How much money does he have? ______________

8. Gretchen has $1,034.60 to pay the following bills: mortgage—$635.50, utilities—$93.29, groceries—$130.25, and credit card payment—$145.38.
   How much is the total? How much will she have left?

Step 1

Mortgage ____________

Utilities ____________

Groceries ____________

Credit card payment ____________

Total expenses ____________

Step 2

Money Gretchen has ____________

Gretchen's total expenses ____________

Cash on hand ____________

Review: Unit 4

REVIEW

Read each problem carefully. Solve it on a separate sheet of paper. Write your answer on the line beside each problem.

1. Maynard has 9 half-dollars, 13 quarters, 21 dimes, 17 nickels, and 39 pennies. How much money does he have? ____________

2. Tracy paid the following bills: rent—$425.50, utilities—$72.54, food—$62.38, and medical bills—$75.50. How much money did she pay? ____________

3. Mr. Sanchez had $210.00 before he went shopping. He now has $97.27. How much money did he spend? ____________

4. Ezio wants to buy a stereo for $365.00. He has $187.65. How much more money does he need? ____________

5. Mr. DiMaria spent $633.00 during the past 12 weeks for office supplies. How much money did he spend each week? ____________

6. Angela saved $106.75 in 5 weeks. How much money did she save each week?

7. Felix saved $26.31 one week, $56.09 the second week, and $30.60 the third week. How much money did he save? ____________

8. Mrs. Jenkins bought 2 9-volt batteries @ $1.89 and 3 rolls of color print film @ $2.99. How much money did she spend? ____________

9. Clifford bought 8 pens @ $1.89, 4 calendars @ $4.49, and 12 message pads @ $.96. How much did he spend? ____________

10. Mrs. Peña charges $110.00 for lawn care and landscaping. He uses half of the money to pay his two employees. How much does each employee earn? ____________

11. A ticket for a concert costs $14.75. What is the cost of

    4 tickets? ____________ 7 tickets? ____________ 15 tickets? ____________

12. A public parking lot charges $2.65 per hour. What will be the parking fee for

    4 hours? ____________ 5 hours? ____________ 15 hours? ____________

TEST

End-of-Book Test

Read each problem carefully. Solve it on a separate sheet of paper. Write your answer on the line beside each problem.

1. Paula wants to buy a microwave oven for $425.00. She has $289.50. How much more money does she need to buy it? ____________

2. The senior class spent $875.00 during the past 14 weeks. How much money did it spend each week? ____________

3. Mr. Carlson bought 8 dictionaries for $191.60. How much money did he pay for each dictionary? ____________

4. Suzette has 9 half-dollars, 13 quarters, 43 dimes, 19 nickels, and 28 pennies. How much money does she have? ____________

5. Maria had $143.00 before she went shopping. She now has $54.07. How much money did she spend? ____________

6. Frank has 41 half-dollars. How much money does he have? ____________

7. Marek saved $45.50 one week, $30.00 the second week, and $50.74 the third week. How much money did he save? ____________

8. Tula had $745.43 in her checking account. She deposited $106.98; then, she wrote a check for $215.37. How much did she have left in her account? ____________

9. Write out in numerals: eight hundred four dollars and five cents. ____________

10. Mr. Marosz has $1,084.53 to pay the following bills: mortgage payment—$650.00, utilities—$98.13, groceries—$81.29, and credit card payment—$152.20. How much is the total? How much money did he have left?

Step 1

Mortgage payment __________

Utility bills __________

Groceries __________

Credit card payment __________

Total expenses __________

Step 2

Money Mr. Marosz had __________

Mr. Marosz's total expenses __________

Cash on hand __________